JOURNAL

21-Day

Weight Release Journey

Create the Best Version of YOU:

Mind, Body & Soul

By Jackie Harden

"May the God of hope fill you with all
joy and peace as you trust in Him, so
that you may overflow with hope by the
power of the Holy Spirit."
~ Romans 15:13 (NIV)

"Wishing you love, peace,
and joy overflowing"
~ Jackie Harden

Table of Contents

Part 3 – The Soul

INTRODUCTION

Thank you for showing up for yourself. Now, get ready to play full-out. Commit to reading one chapter each day of the "21-Day Weight Release Journey: Create the Best Version of YOU: Mind, Body & Soul" and complete the journal exercises here in your personal journal. Be honest with yourself. Write down what comes up for you and invite someone to share this journey with you. For best results, join the free Facebook Group "Best Life Creators" to connect with others who are on this journey as well. Having a supportive community will help you stay on track and can also make this journey a lot of fun.

Enjoy the process.

SPIRIT
RELATIONSHIP WITH GOD
HOPE
OBEDIENCE
FAITH
HUMILITY
HEALING
MIND
THOUGHTS
WORDS
WHAT WE SEE AND HEAR
ATTITUDE
BODY
HOW WE TAKE CARE OF OUR BODIES
WHAT WE PUT INTO OUR BODIES

PART 1

THE MIND

Day 1: The Power of Your Mind

"Whatsoever things are true, whatsoever things are honest, whatsoever things are just, whatsoever things are pure, whatsoever things are lovely, whatsoever things are of good report, if there be any virtue, and if there be any praise, think on these things." ~ Philippians 4:8

It has been said that what we think about, we bring about. Another way of saying that is what our mind conceives, and we believe, we will achieve. The mind is extremely powerful, and we must consciously feed it positive information in order to reap a positive result.

Journal Activity #1: Think about your positive attributes. What have you accomplished in the past? Think about a time when you felt good. What was going on around you? How did you feel inside? What happened that contributed to your state of happiness, well-being, and joy? What do you want more of in your life right now? What will it take to make it happen? What are the steps to get there? Write it out, step by step.

Here's an affirmation for today: "I am worthy of my goals, dreams, and desires."

Whatever you want to achieve over the next 21 days, tell yourself every morning and every night before you go to sleep "I am worthy of ...." Fill in the blank with the thing you intend to be, do, or have.

____

____

____

____

____

____

____

____

____

____

____

____

____

____

____

____

____

____

____

____

____

____

____

____

"Mind power is one of the strongest and most useful powers you possess. This power, together with your imagination, can create success or failure, happiness or unhappiness, opportunities or obstacles." ~ Joseph Murphy

Day 2: Subconscious Mind vs. Conscious Mind

"Your mind is alert; your memory is keen for you have the all-knowing mind of infinite intelligence within you." ~ Anonymous

<u>**Journal Activity #2:**</u> Write down three gratitude statements you will tell yourself today. Start first thing in the morning. And create three powerful statements that you want for your life.

For example, I am happy, healthy, and financially abundant. I release all struggle and anxiety for I know God is with me always. I release my fear of lack and accept the abundance and prosperity of the universe.

____

____

____

____

____

____

____

Day 3: The Power of Focused Intention

"Intention is a force in the universe, and everything and everyone is connected to this invisible force."
~ Dr. Wayne W. Dyer

<u>Journal Activity #3:</u> Write five gratitude statements and set your intentions for your day and night's sleep. What will you focus on? Choose an area of your life and write down what you are willing to create. What is your primary focus for your life right now? What is your utmost desire?

____

____

____

____

____

____

____

____

Day 4: Think Big

**"As a man thinketh in his heart,
so is he." ~ Proverbs 23:7**

<u>Journal Activity #4:</u> Write five gratitude statements and set your intentions for your day and night's sleep. What will you focus on? Choose an area of your life and write down what you are willing to create. What is your primary focus for your life right now? What is your utmost desire? THINK BIG!

____

____

____

____

____

____

____

____

Day 5: Miracle Working Power

"Do not be anxious about anything, but in every situation, by prayer and petition, with thanksgiving, present your requests to God. And the peace of God, which transcends all understanding, will guard your hearts and your minds in Christ Jesus." ~ Philippians 1:6-7

Journal Activity #5: Consider the following questions and write about what comes up for you: What are you holding on to that no longer serves a positive purpose in your life? When you release it, what will you create in its place? When it comes to holding on to something or someone that doesn't serve your greater good, just know that it is taking up space for something else (something better). It is acting as a distraction or is blocking you from experiencing something greater.

Make deep breathing, prayer and meditation a part of your daily routine and notice how you feel. Then write about it in your journal.

____

____

____

Day 6: Powerful Conversations

"What other people think of me is none of my business."
~ Eleanor Roosevelt

Journal Activity #6: Create positive affirmations for yourself or use the ones provided above. Write them on post-it notes, and post them on the bathroom mirror, near your computer at work, or on the dashboard of your car. Post them anywhere you are sure to notice them, so you are reminded of your greatness. Say them in the morning and all throughout the day. Continue to write at least five gratitude statements every day.

Here are some of the affirmations I use daily. Try using these affirmations or create some of your own.

I am Happy.
I am Healthy, Wealthy, and Wise.
I am Secure.
I am Worthy.
I am Positive.
I am Beautiful, Loved, and Blessed.
I am Grateful.
I am Confident.
I am Courageous.
I am Excited About Today.

Day 7: Declare Your Victory

**"Whatever you declare for your life and
take action to manifest will happen."
~ Jackie Harden**

How has the first week of this journey been for you? Are you seeing results? Are you staying in action? Do you need to make adjustments to get on track to achieve your goal? What is your plan of action? Are you implementing it? Are there any obstacles standing in your way? What steps are you willing to take to remove all distractions, obstacles, and excuses. What do you need help with? Who can you ask to support you? Focus on the goal.

Right here right now declare your victory!

Journal Activity #7: Write the answers to the questions above. Write about how you will feel when you achieve your goal. Be descriptive. Celebrate your progress. Notice what you are thinking, feeling, and experiencing. Stay in gratitude!

____

____

____

____

Part 2

THE BODY

Day 8: Your Body is a Temple

"Know ye not that your body is the temple of the Holy Ghost, which is in you..."
~ 1 Corinthians 6:19

Your body is a gift from God.

What you do with it is your gift to God.

__Journal Activity #8:__ Write five gratitude statements for and about your body. Then decide what action you will take to improve your health and well-being.

____

____

____

____

____

____

____

Day 9: You Are in Control of Your Physical Body

"A healthy mindset is a key component to a healthy body." ~ Inc.com

<u>Journal Activity #9</u>: Continue stating affirmations to uplift your spirit. What actions will you take today to care for yourself? Be kind to yourself and do something nice for yourself (i.e., soak in the tub, dance, go for a walk). Then write about how caring for yourself made you feel.

____

____

____

____

____

____

____

____

____

Day 10: Your Body's Response to Weight

**"A heart at peace gives life to the body,
but envy rots the bones."
~ Proverbs 14:30**

<u>Journal Activity #10</u>: Here are questions to help you release the weight. Is there anything you would do differently if you had the chance? It is said that we are as sick as our secrets. What secrets are you keeping? What does it cost you to keep those secrets? How honest are you willing to be with yourself and others to achieve the peace of mind you deserve?

____

____

____

____

____

____

____

____

Day 11: The Choice is Yours

"The ultimate measure of a man is not where he stands in moments of comfort and convenience, but where he stands in times of challenge and controversy." ~ Martin L. King, Jr.

<u>**Journal Activity #11**</u>: Today, take time to write a Love Letter to yourself. Show yourself love for who you are and what you've accomplished thus far in life. Who will you commit to being and what will you commit to doing, to have the life you know you deserve? The choice is yours to release the weight and take action to create the best version of yourself one day at a time.

Reminder: If you always do, what you've always done. You'll always get what you've always gotten.

____

____

____

____

____

____

Day 12: Be Bold About Getting Unblocked

**"Be bold and mighty forces will
come to your aid." ~ Basil King**

<u>Journal Activity #12</u>: Take a look at where you are now and where you would like to be. If you knew you couldn't fail, what would you do differently? How would life be for you if you released the weight you've been holding onto? What do you want to change in your life, and how would life be if you made those changes? What's the vision for your life? What does it look like? What does it feel like? Can you visualize the life you want to create? After writing the answers to these questions, create a vision board. Put everything you want and know you deserve on the board.

Day 13: Press Forward – No Matter What!

"This one thing I do, forgetting those things which are behind, and reaching forth unto those things which are before, I press toward the mark for the prize of the high calling of God" ~ Philippians 3:13-14

<u>**Journal Activity #13**</u>: Show gratitude for the battles you have faced, fought, and overcome, which brought you to where you are now. Declare for yourself that you will not give up on your dreams, goals, and desires. What action will you take today to move closer to your goal?

"Never let success get to your head; never let failure get to your heart."
~ Anonymous

____

____

____

____

____

____

Day 14: Stay in Action

"We are what we repeatedly do. Excellence, then, is not an act but a habit." ~ Aristotle

<u>**Journal Activity #14:**</u> Stay in action. Consistent Small Wins Create Big Wins! Write about the action you have taken thus far on this journey and the results you've gotten. If you haven't taken action, notice what you've been telling yourself and take action to change the conversation to one that is empowering, uplifting, and will motivate you to action. Research your field of interest to find out what resources are available.

____

____

____

____

____

____

____

____

**"Now faith is the substance of things hoped for and the
evidence of things not seen."
~ Hebrews 11:1**

Part 3

THE SOUL

Day 15: "Stretch Out on Faith and Let the Miracle Happen" ~ Jackie Harden

Journal Activity #15: Write about one thing you keep putting off. What's holding you back? What do you fear? What has the fear, doubt, and procrastination cost you? And, what has to happen for you to stretch out on faith to remove that mountain?

____

____

____

____

____

____

____

____

Day 16: What Do You Believe?

"Belief comes before the victory."
~ Anonymous

<u>Journal Activity #16</u>: Write about your experience on this 21-Day Journey. Are you making progress? What is your mindset? Are you staying in gratitude? Are you staying in action? Have you committed yourself to repeat powerful affirmations daily? What do you believe about yourself and your ability to achieve your goal?

____

____

____

____

____

____

____

____

____

Day 17: Search Your Soul

"Your role is to do you so well that you SHIFT your own history and come into the mystery of an unfolding soul that is always just getting started." ~ Michael Beckwith

<u>**Journal Activity #17**</u>: Take inventory of your life. What have you already overcome? What goals have you already achieved? What have you learned from your past experiences? Challenging experiences help to develop character and resilience. What have you learned about yourself? How can this information serve you right now and prepare you for the life you are creating?

____

____

____

____

____

____

____

Day 18: Surrender to Spirit

**"I am the way, the truth and the life:
no [wo]man cometh unto the Father but by me."
~ John 14:6**

<u>Journal Activity #18</u>: What can you experience if/when you decide to let go and turn your struggle over to Spirit. What will you have space for when you release the weight? Surrender to the Spirit and soar.

____

____

____

____

____

____

____

____

____

____

Day 19: Tell the Truth

**"The voice of truth speaks to us
every single day and it is as loud as
our willingness to listen.
Your dark chapter is not the whole book."
~ Mary Morrissey**

<u>Journal Activity #19</u>: Tell your story. What have you done? Where have you been? Who have you loved? Who have you lost? Who have you hurt? Who have you helped? Do you see the value in self-love? Why is self-love important? Validate every aspect of your being. You matter! Every part of your story matters! What do you want the next chapter of your life to look like? What do you want to create now? Write it all out. Tell the truth!

____

____

____

____

____

____

____

Day 20: Love is an Action Word

**"Love is patient and kind, love is not envious, or
boastful or arrogant or rude. It does not insist
on its own way, it is not irritable or resentful.
It does not rejoice in wrongdoing,
but rejoices in the truth.
Love never ends."
~ Corinthians 13:4-8**

<u>**Journal Activity #20:**</u> If you want love, be loving.
Think about love today and show love for yourself
and others. In so doing, what did you discover?
What's your definition of love? How do you express
love? How is your love life? How would you like
your love life to be? How can you elevate and create
more love in your life?

**"God so loved the world that He gave His only
begotten son that whosoever believeth in Him
should not perish but have everlasting life."
~ John 3:16**

____

____

____

____

____

Day 21: We Get the Life We Create

**"We don't get the life we deserve.
We get the life we create."
~ Anonymous**

Congratulations!
You made it to day 21!

Journal Activity #21: Assess your progress. What did you want to achieve during this 21 Day Journey and what did you accomplish? Did you write in your journal every day? Did you complete the journal exercises each day? Look back on your journal entries and notice your mind set, notice the thoughts, behaviors, and actions that you wrote about in your journal. Where are you now compared to where you began 21 days ago?

Celebrate your successes!

____

____

____

____

____

Visit www.jackieharden.com to download your free gift, "**Overcoming Limiting Beliefs**" and to learn more about Jackie's programs and offerings. You can also connect with her on social media:

- *https://www.facebook.com/jaciehardenlifecoach*
- *https://www.instagram.com/jackievharden*
- *https://www.linkedin.com/in/jackievharden*

Facebook Group "Best Life Creators"
www.facebook.com/groups/2627635074217340/